# COFFEE SHOP

## Aaron Lebold

BLOOD MOON POETRY

Uncomfortably Dark Horror

Copyright © 2025 Coffee Shop by Aaron Lebold

All rights reserved.

No part of this publication may be reproduced, distributed, or transmitted in any form or by any means, including photocopying, recording, or other electronic or mechanical methods, without the prior written permission of the publisher, except as permitted by U.S. copyright law. For permission requests, contact editor@uncomfortablydark.com.

The story, all names, characters, and incidents portrayed in this production are fictitious. No identification with actual persons (living or deceased), places, buildings, and products is intended or should be inferred.

Book Cover by Ruth Anna Evans

Interior photo by Aaron Lebold

First edition 2025

Edited & formatted by 360 Editing, a division of Uncomfortably Dark Horror.

Editor: Candace Nola

Published by Uncomfortably Dark Horror, owned and operated by Candace Nola. Pittsburgh, PA

Follow us on all social media, our Patreon, or on our website to stay up to date on new releases, appearances, and more!

Committed to *"bringing you the best in horror, one uncomfortably dark page at a time."*

*Patreon*

Website

# Contents

| | |
|---|---|
| Dedication | VII |
| 1. Part 1 | 1 |
| 2. Part 2 | 17 |
| 3. Part 3 | 28 |
| 4. Part 4 | 45 |
| 5. Part 5 | 61 |
| 6. Part 6 | 70 |
| 7. Part 7 | 83 |
| Also by Aaron Lebold | 87 |
| About the author | 88 |

## Early Praise for Coffee Shop

*"A poignant rumination about growth and self-reflection that will inspire and infuriate with its honesty."*—Patrick Tumblety, author of COME OUT & PLAY

*"A brilliant collection, filled with both darkness and luminosity. Rhythmic, evocative, and an absolutely satisfying experience. Highly recommended!"*—Brian Bowyer, Author of OLD TOO SOON

*A collected book of poetry, and journal entries, from my youth.*

# DEDICATION

*This book is dedicated to anyone who feels a constant need for growth and self-awareness. Change is hard, but not as hard as staying the same.*

# Part 1

---

Before even writing my first word, I already know. This may as well have been written on a typewriter in a coffee shop. Poetry has always been bittersweet to me. I began writing as a teenager. I never really thought of it as writing; I thought of it as creating songs. Lyrics to inspire others the way that I had been inspired.

It turned out music was never really my niche. So here we are. On the flip side of that, a lot of poetry people annoy me. It's effortless to string some vague phrases together and try to convince others that you're deep. That you have a soul. That you have something to say. I feel like that is what I'm about to do. May as well put on my fedora and head to the coffee shop with my typewriter.

Condemn me as I condemn myself. Judge me as I dive headfirst into a cliché that has always felt like hollow ghosts trying to create the illusion that they have a soul. Maybe to convince themselves, maybe to convince others, maybe just because they are lost. I know exactly where I'm going, but I've never felt more lost. I have a beautiful woman above me on the next floor who makes me feel something I haven't felt for a long time, if ever.

I feel something genuine. Honest. I also feel sad because I know she is going to do amazing things, and I won't be there to see it. I miss her before she's even gone. I know she's going to go because she has to. She cares for me enough to hold me accountable for what I told her I wanted months ago. I need to find myself as an individual. I need to be okay with being alone.

She needs the same thing. So, the connection that we have will eventually be broken. I know it's going to hurt, but I'm learning how to change that. She's teaching me. She is beautiful in every sense of the word. She deserves a poem, so here we are, at the coffee shop.

---

I know the way you feel; your world is falling down

Everything you know, your union with the clown

Please do not believe the picture that he paints

You are like his drug, only nice tits and restraints

There is a beauty in you that was broken in your youth

He saw that as an opportunity to shape you into something shapeless

To keep you broken so that you would cope in the only way that you knew how

By making yourself feel like you only mean something with your clothes off

As soon as you wake up, I'd like to lay you on the floor

Hide out in the basement, be sure to close the door

Take my time and do the thing I'm not supposed to do

Allowing sex to mean something, mean something with you

Four months of getting to know you, the real you

Having someone to talk to about me, the real me

I'm still learning how to separate sex from love, fun from connection

You have been the best teacher I could have ever asked for, but this will hurt

I see through your eyes; I know how you feel

The spirit inside you is broken but real

I wish you could see the courage you hold

I hope more than that — that you don't quit and fold

It is now three-thirty-six in the morning.

I know you had a rough day, and you look so peaceful when you sleep, but it's time to wake you up.

Everything is done, and if I'm completely honest, I'm afraid that after tonight I may lose you.

I know I'll still see you, but I know you're going to pull away.

You're going to keep your promise and force me into the shadows.

I'm going to miss you more than you will probably ever know, even if I see you again, even if we still have sex.

Tonight, I want to give in to my impulses, and I want to allow you to feel like my world.

I want to show you how much you have meant to me.

You are the best person that could have possibly come into my life at the exact time I needed it.

I didn't even know I needed you.

I love you.

---

***I wrote this when I was young, I'm not sure exactly when.***

Don't bother to sing to me

Some gut-wrenching lullaby

Don't bother wasting your time

Listening to me cry

I promise I won't dwell on your absence

## COFFEE SHOP

I promise I won't mimic your fear

I promise I won't question your judgment

In your presence, I will not shed a tear

Look at our cute little baby

Our tiny, blue-eyed little son

Soon he's gonna grow up tall

He'll grow up to be what we know he will be

He'll grow up to be a disappointment

A disappointment

A disappointment

A disappointment

---

Slowly losing touch with reality

Can't come to grips with your vanity

Take me down brick by brick, with silence

Show me how you feel with violence

Falling apart

Desperately seeking understanding

Talk to me

Stop the silence

Show me that I'm not a fool

Tell me I'm not wasting my time

Keeping me in the dark until I rot

Mold and mildew cover the plot

How will the story end?

Happily ever after, or defamation to defend?

Show me who you are

I don't want to guess; it's gone too far

Turn on the light, let me out of the dark

It's peaceful and silent, but I still see the shark

---

### *From my journal...*

I need your help now; I know you always know what's going to happen,

but as of now I really don't see the point of this.

Trust me, I am kind of done here because I really need to know.

Please

Please

Please

Please

Please

Please

Please

Please

Please

PLEASE

You better fucking know what you're doing or I'll kill both of us.

Think I'm fucking lying? Do you?

Where are you?

Fuck you.

How can I trust you?

How can I trust again anymore?

I don't even know you

Did these pills kill you?

NO. NO.

---

You spent so many years playing me with your games

Now I try not to laugh as it goes down in flames

You can blame me if you want, but you did it to yourself

Your deceit now is over, placed high up on the shelf

Closure was much bigger than I thought

I'll bet you never would have guessed that you'd get caught

It's over now, time to go

It's all come down, and you should know

I've spent too much time feeling sorry for myself

And just enough time subconsciously plotting my revenge

I think it's over now

At least it's close

No one to talk to

No one to blame but myself

No faith to call my own

No choice but to be alone

No way to kill the demon

Love is nothing more than sweat and semen

Maybe it is time to call it quits

Maybe time for some deeper slits

## COFFEE SHOP

---

There is no real closure yet

You haven't beaten shit

You are just at the beginning of your long journey

That will eventually lead to death

Still, you carry on because you have to

Is she real?

I have doubts. I have doubts about everything.

About reality

People

Sanity

If I can't trust the people that say they love me, who can I trust?

Definitely not myself

I'm lost

They know what they're doing, and they know how to get the best of me

They know how to break me down

I am weak, but I am strong. I will defeat them.

I will kill the demon

Can love kill the demon?

Is there love?

Is there a demon?

Of course. He's in your head. You can beat him.

Lie back and relax; it will only hurt for a second

You'll get used to it. You already are.

So numb. So dead.

A robot programmed to do what I tell it to do.

You are a puppet, but you will get your success

You will be remembered

You are completely fucking insane, kid.

I know because I am your insanity

I am your demon

Don't try to kill me because I am a gift

You need me

You're nothing by yourself

When I go away is when you want to die

You have to accept me; you can't beat me, and I haven't steered you wrong yet

Don't waste your time trying to figure it out

The pieces will fall into place over time

Everything happens for a reason, and that reason is me

Keep your eyes open, watch; I'll show you what's important

Like I always have

I'm here to help you. I am your angel. I'm not a demon.

Don't suppress me.

Don't get help. They can't help you.

Don't talk to them; talk to me

They don't understand; they are selfish

Follow my voice; believe me. Trust me.

You're not alone, and you don't need flesh for companionship

This is a valuable lesson

Stick to your ground and don't let them get the best of you

You've dealt with stronger, smarter, meaner, and won

Stick with me, we'll make it to the grave.

Peacefully

---

You have to help me. I know it's part of the process, but it hurts.

Trust me

I know. I'm sorry. I just feel so lost.

Sometimes, you're the only one I trust. I need you.

I know you do. We'll get through this.

We always do, and it will all make sense.

It will all make sense later.

---

A friend with weed is a friend indeed

A friend with heroin is better

It's been so long since we reached the end

I really miss you, my old friend

I have new friends, but they aren't the same

They make me numb, but there's still pain

I wish you could come back to me

That all could be as it used to be

---

Once upon a time, sobriety was reality

Those days have come and gone

## COFFEE SHOP

Everyday life contained consistency

Feels like it's been so long

Then I found a way to make it easy

Found a way to numb the pain

A simple powder that could appease me

Creativity seemed to be my gain

---

Remembering the drug

Trying to pick up the pieces

Trying to sort things out

It's been so many years

Since I've been face to face with doubt

I used to have my systems

I used to have my ways

I had all my little tricks to make it through the days

I numbed it, hid it away

Put it off for another day

I have to remember the method

I have to remember the way

I have to remember the drug

That used to get me day to day

It was creation

It was an outlet

It was melody and rhythm

Music was the drug

Music was the drug

Music was the drug

---

Hidden spark, somewhere in the dark

You have to come back

You were always there for me before

Did I kill you with heroin and morphine?

I'm sorry; it was so hard, and now I'm alone again

Like I'm sure you knew I would be

Please

I need your help

I need to remember who I am

I need to remember how to deal with this fucking noise in my head

Alcohol doesn't work; I just make an ass of myself and come home and cut my wrist open

Any night I go to the bar, I'm wondering if I can sort my shit out

If I can be seen as a normal person

I want this noise to go away

You know how to filter it

Come back

Please come back

I can't do this without you

I just can't

Fact

---

Rejected, denied, fucked up again

Can't help but feel that this may be the end

How much longer can I pretend?

How much longer until the end?

Put me out of my misery

Kill me, kill me, kill me, kill me, kill me, kill me

Help me, help me

Fuck, I give up

---

*EMPTY AND ALONE*

*EMPTY AND ALONE*

*EMPTY AND ALONE*

*EMPTY AND ALONE*

# Part 2

***Back in the coffee shop – Present time***

Sitting here, I adjust my fedora and glance around the room to make sure people are looking at me. Perceiving me as a complicated enigma, pouring out his very soul through his fingertips as they dance on the typewriter keys. I think of you. I've been thinking of you every time I speak with my lawyer. Every time I see shit on the ground. I think of you.

I'm going to do my best to write my feelings about you in a beautiful string of words. For you, words are weapons. For me, words are a gateway to a world you will never be capable of understanding. That's the thing about narcissism. You don't have any real feelings, you just latch on to people and try to mimic theirs. I would feel bad about you, but I can't. Empathy is my greatest strength, and when I try to put myself in your mind, I feel nothing. I feel emptiness. I see things through your eyes, and all I can think of doing is playing the game. To completely crush you, just like I told myself months ago when this all began.

I don't want to write a poem about you. I don't want you to think that you are going to be remembered. As soon as we finish our dance with the house and the lawyers, you will disappear. By this time next year, I probably won't even remember your middle name. The one thing you kept telling me was that you hoped I wasn't with you because it felt like where I was supposed to be. A lesson I was supposed to learn. It always was. I always knew it on some level. There were so many red flags, and I kept going. Not because I didn't see them, but because I ignored them, knowing that it would make sense at some point. It makes sense now. Thank you for the lesson. I'm feeling much more confident in myself, and the battle with you has been a big part of that.

You, as a person, are irrelevant. You don't matter. You are pathetic and weak, and you're going to end up surrounded by burned bridges, sitting in a trailer with nobody in your life that wants to deal with you. Just like your biological mother. Nature vs. nurture. You'll never see it, but you already are a spitting image.

You don't make me angry, not anymore. After I stood on that cliff in Portugal, and I saw that you wouldn't even consider doing the smallest thing to offer me a spark of happiness, I couldn't deny it anymore. I didn't care. You never did. You proved that day after day after I liberated myself from you. You proved that without a doubt when we saw the most useless counsellor I've ever seen. When I saw you manipulate her and lie, I saw the game you were playing. You didn't care about us; you cared about keeping the illusion that you were right. You cared about the life that I gave you, that you felt you deserved to

# COFFEE SHOP

keep if I was in it or not. I saw the game you played and lowered myself to your level to play along.

Since then, it's been a journey of self-awareness. Seeing the world through your eyes, with no emotion and no regard for how much I may hurt you in the process of destroying your ego. I've never been able to do that before. Stay completely selfish and not get stuck in the trap of caring. It's been challenging, but this lesson is one that I could never have learned without you. I appreciate that. But it could have been any narcissist; don't get the impression that you're special. You're a dime a dozen.

***"What a long, strange trip it's been..."***

---

Why hello, I see we meet again

You think you got me this time?

I'm back up on my feet

You cannot make this end

You sure hit hard, but I'm a great defender

You always hit where it hurts, kick me when I'm down

But do you really think I'll ever surrender?

Push me down and drag me around

Stomp my head down into the ground

As close as I come

As close as I've came

Never will I die

Never will I play your game

---

Three stood up, three fell down

Wipe all the blood off your clean white gown

The first was a killer; the second cut deep

The third was the hardest, a solitary leap

You three deceiving soldiers have taught me quite well

Now I think I am ready, but only time will tell

We will hang the fourth soldier who draws out their sword

Strung up in the branches in front of their Lord

I warn you, fourth soldier, your fate is not fun

If you hear my warning, you should turn and run

My mind, it can slip only so far

My eyes open wide, and I see who you are

Your cover's transparent; I see your heart's black

My head has transformed; there are eyes in the back

The winds, they will shift, and your cover will spoil

## COFFEE SHOP

My anger will flourish if you make it boil

As the hands on the clock move slowly ahead

Your manipulation becomes as good as dead

You'll be blown wide open, we'll see your true face

Your wretched betrayal, your chilling embrace

You'll turn and you'll run, you'll target the door

But before you arrive, you're a spot on the floor

---

It's getting hard to handle you

You're difficult to put faith into

Try to pretend, I reach for my drawer

As soon as I'm high, I'm down on the floor

Deteriorating options getting hard to hide

The knots and pains end up inside

Oh, to be ignorant, day by day

Not understanding a thing that you say

Living life without question

Oversee all inquiries to mention

Why can't I use you the way you use me?

Why can't I believe everything that I see?

Why must I notice all the pieces don't fit?

Why can't I just be happy with it?

Why can't people not just be who they say?

Why are they acting, day after day?

Put an awful lot of energy into being lazy

Just come clean; my vision's getting hazy

---

Drinking water

Same old shit from day to day

Need someone to show me the way

Same old, same old, in despair

Same old, same old, I don't care

What I need is peace of mind

A little change from chains that bind

Restitution from myself

Or a bullet leaving its shell

It comes from everyone; it comes from everywhere

You may not know it, but you have your share

It knows our weaknesses, but it doesn't bother

It just seeps into our drinking water

Right into the drinking water

---

All About The Love

Possible solutions for a definite problem

I think it's time to fly

Fly far away from here

Leave your memory for death

I don't want it anymore

You've soiled it

All the purity gone

I can't believe how much of me I gave to you

How pathetic

What a waste

I'm so ashamed

You are such a disappointment

Or maybe just the thought

Perhaps I always knew

Kept it suppressed, buried deep

I guess I gave too much, too much faith

Or maybe I just needed someone to hold, to talk to

To keep me pure

It's all about the love, all about the hate, all about the habits that you just can't break

All about the look that's in your eye, all about the urge that I have to die

All about the drugs that keep me sane, all about the demons in my brain

I wish the world would stop spinning

Because I'm getting dizzy

I know me so much better now

Do I have you to thank?

Or was it inevitable?

You're going to get what you're after

But you'll never get me back

I see you for you, behind wasted eyes

So high, yet so low

Do I feel this because of you?

Or is it just the drugs?

I don't think it even matters

You won't get out of my head, why?

I can't help but be disappointed, ashamed, frustrated, and hate us both with a passion

But sometimes, sometimes I'm okay

Other times I'm dead; other times I'm alive

Confusion. Are you confused?

I don't think you are. I think you're simple.

Black and white imposter, I think you're shallow

I don't miss you at all, but I cared so much

For that feeling. You. Drugs. Pseudo happiness.

I'm so empty. You drained what was left.

You set me free, I'm free, watch me fly

Not held back anymore

I love you; I hate you; you mean everything to me

I don't miss you a bit; I can't live without you

Thank you. Fuck you.

Help me. Go away. Goodbye.

---

Hesitate

Another night to remember, a few more things to forget

Throw these feelings in the pile, move on without regret

Walking backwards through time, but here I am, still technically fine

You smashed the window of opportunity; you broke in and stole the TV

I won't hesitate to kill you

I won't hesitate to make you bleed

You are strong, but you are lacking

You don't understand the hate you feed

Haven't been outside, no need for sunscreen

All I've had to eat today is morphine

Tired of promises turning to lies

Sick of hellos turning into goodbyes

I'm sick of feeling possessed, like a pet

Sick of you showing now and then, saying, not yet

Sick of conversations behind my back

Sick of my world in pieces, when it once was intact

I'm sick of the future turning into the past

I'm sick of these things being too good to last

Sick of you contradicting your cases,

Sick of the sight of no mind and two faces

## COFFEE SHOP

I'm sick of the earth and the sun spinning 'round

I'm sick of the sky, the stars, and the ground

I'm sick of the trees, the water, the air

Sick of everything, everyone, everywhere

I'm sick of you saying what's wrong and what's right

I'm sick of what's arid, what's damp, dark and light

I'm sick of the way that you look down on me

Sick of you saying how it will be

Sick of you judging every part of my life

Sick of your spoon, your fork, and your knife

I'm sick of the way that you pick things apart

I'm sick of you shitting and calling it art

I'm sick of what's right, sick of what's wrong

Sick of your world, sick of this song

# Part 3

***Well, that was another jaded journal from the depths of my youth. Welcome back to the coffee shop.***

Since you left, there have been some new developments. I can admit when I'm wrong, and I would like a do-over.

These are my new plans for tonight.

---

I shouldn't be surprised; you did what you said you would do

I shouldn't be upset; I was never supposed to get attached to you

# COFFEE SHOP

I was never really mad, but I really was hurt

Shouldn't be a shock, based on the way that you flirt

I just don't understand why you let me fall in love

It felt more like a stab when it should have been a shove

We took it as close to the edge as it would go

That was the nature of us, that we both know

But when it came to a close, and you made your choice

Instead of your body, I wish you used your voice

I never thought we would go our separate ways

But I'm starting to heal, I guess solitude pays

I guess I should thank you, even though it's been hell

It's exactly what I needed. I hope you're doing well.

I want to remember our time with a smile

Still a bit jaded, that may take a while

So, my plans for tonight? I may need to think.

Maybe have a fire, smoke cigarettes, and drink

---

Oh, the guilt.

He believed himself to be a diamond in the rough

He looked for support; they said he wasn't enough

Each day, like the last, always trying to please

But it was never enough; he could never appease

Try as he might, he always fell short

People shooting him down as if it were sport

No matter how many times he was put in his place

He always had a part of his mind up in space

Never seem to be good enough for you

Oh, the guilt

Always fall short despite how much I do

Oh, the guilt

All the dreams you've had will now never be

Oh, the guilt

And obviously it's because of me

Oh, the guilt

Just as time and time before, he tries again

He will try and try and try until the end

He gathers all his courage and he gets up on stage

He can barely read the words on the page

He hopes all he knows that he is will prevail

He hopes that his train of thought does not derail

# COFFEE SHOP

He pretends he's just at home, gives it all that he's got

Because of all he knows, this is his only shot

Seems to be a mixed reaction, half and half

Some think it's good, some think it sucks, some laugh

All this time inside his mind, he's been so sure

Kept himself on track, kept himself pure

Now everything that he knew has turned into doubt

He questions everything that he has ever felt

Where he goes from here, he does not know

The path is long and hard, have to take it slow.

---

I am in hysterics, laughing 'till I bleed

You've all made me realize exactly what I need

The cobwebs have cleared, I remember myself

Take all your regrets; keep them to yourself

My strength has returned; my head is all clear

And it's all 'cause you fucked me into the right year

Keep an eye on your karma; it never forgets

Look at the big picture, and see your regrets

You took it too far; you cannot turn back

You were all blind to the knowledge you lack

The thought may have hit you, but now it's too late

Emotions too strong and the thought far too great

Loving the freedom of being alone

You've made your decisions, now you're on your own

I don't need you; I'm fine as it stands

And you'll never clean the dirt from your hands.

---

Breaking Point

Pulsating vein at the side of my head, heart beating faster, face turning red

Laugh again, grate my nerves. Say it all, find the words.

Take another shot at my life, treat me like a bitch as you put the knife

Deeper in my back, I simply welcome your attack

Mock my values, spit in my face, rub it all in, keep me down in my place

Hit all of my buttons with all of your force, devalue me without any remorse

One more step

## COFFEE SHOP

One more crack

One more inch

One more lie

Over the edge

Shattered and smashed,

Kill you all, breaking point

Breaking point

Leave me the fuck alone

This and that, this and that,

Constant screaming from the fucking cat

Crazy lady, freezing cold.

Clean this, clean that, do what you're told.

Repeat it forty times cause I'm fucking dumb.

I'm terribly sorry now I get it, Mom.

Your life is so hard, and I've got it made.

Twenty hours a week in the grocery store just to get paid

All I have to do is drive down the street

Spend nine hours a day moving concrete

Can I please just get a little fucking respect?

You've got your reasons, that I accept.

I've had to earn everything that I own.

You think that I'm shit, so just leave me alone.

I'm so sick of this shit, no help at all.

A million boots will kick me when I finally fall.

The life that I seek is not a lot to ask,

Some peace and quiet and to hide in my mask

I know the way it works; you have to pay to play.

You've got a lot to do, so just fucking go away.

---

Obituary

I'm always so sure

I'm always so wrong

Did I move too fast?

or did I take too long?

Or is it just me?

Obituary

So close, did you smell death?

That's my cologne

The smell of destitution, forever alone

I know I'm hard to handle

I can't handle me

Soon I'll cross the line

So I can be free

Obituary

Was it something I said, or was it just me?

I guess you're page four of the eulogy

I can't find the answers that will sedate me.

All in all you're all my

Obituary

---

Lemmings...

There is a truth hidden under the skin. I close my eyes; my world begins to spin.

There is an apple in reach, as I take a bite, you begin to teach.

Everything is not what it seems. Skin covers all the soulless machines.

Flex your pecs and take your keratein, we all get in line to stick our heads in the guillotine.

It's a plastic world, and it's almost too late,

Your credit card will determine your fate.

Take a few lines, take a look around.

Take a few pills, take hold of the sound.

There is a life behind the star, a whole new world behind the wheel of that car.

Do you believe in destiny? I'm still trying to conquer all my hatred and jealousy.

What's the worst thing that a boy could do? It's all fun and games until he's after you.

Just sit back and watch the sin fall. It's bound to happen, and we're all dead after all.

Think they'll ever find the cure? When nature does the crime, murder is pure.

There's guilt written all over your face. Say a few words, never beat the disgrace.

Who came up with this plan? Would it be so hard to find a better man?

Now through the rubble we sift,

A pack of lemmings jumping over a cliff.

---

Go

You don't like the way that I live—Go

You don't want what I've got to give—Go

Why are you standing around—Go

Why are you wasting our time—Go

You don't have shit to say—Go

Why are you running away—Go

I think it's time; we can't rewind

Time has passed, couldn't last

Maybe you should. Maybe I should. I think we all should.

Go

I'll earn my own ticket to fly—Go

I'll earn my own freedom to die—Go

Season to season, month to month—Go

I'm driving on something more than a hunch—Go

Lyrical garble and tedious rhyme—Go

The down is there, stop wasting my time—Go

---

LSDimension…

Lifted me up and took me so high, teaching me both how to live and to fly

Lifted me up over mountains and trees, flooding the deserts and drying the seas

Conquer the world as I save all the ashes, self-crowned king as I give them all lashes

Listening with a watchful ear, hearing out all my reasons to die

Judge the world as I tell my story, because Sunday morning brings morning glory

I hid myself in an LSDimension and I never wanted to come down

I hid my life and my misleading complexion in hopes that they would never be found

Tripping away in an LSDimension, trying to forget who I am

Feeling so high above the world, not knowing that it was a scam

Hit after hit, a continuous miss, mind slipping away in a feeling of bliss

Paranoid and confused, what's going on? In feelings of heaven, where did I go wrong?

The mind is a puzzle; the world is a maze; analyze and interpret as nights turn to days

Spirits get broken, minds tend to slip, for a few nights of feeling you're steering the ship

A brutal victim of my own attack, I have no regrets, but I can never go back

Feeling burnt out, but I still needed more, still incomplete, what am I searching for?

It gave me the life that I wanted to live, but it gave me the thoughts of my body to give

My subconscious mind still on my side, keeping me honest, with hope, and alive

I still remember that which I am. I know what you're doing. I won't be your lamb.

You can't take my purity, can't take my dreams, and everything now will go back as it seems.

---

The irony of the word civilization makes me laugh silently to myself

There's something about the way that you belittle me, something much like my fading mental health

Something about the way we keep on fighting, dragging our children down for the likes of greed

The children are unwanted, but yet you love to breed

Close the books on civilization, pounds itself into the ground

Descending as we speak, so much further. Always lost and never found.

Pack your bags and leave for civilization; it's there you'll find the keys to life

Spawn, mate, reproduce and die. Dull the blade and throw the knife

These past few days I've forced myself to ponder, if my dreams are worth a thing

No one else is gonna do it for you, but what's the point of anything?

Put your life into a special project, somewhere that you feel that you belong

Accomplishment feels so far from reach, yet still I carry on

Civil rights and civil wars

Civil strip clubs, civil whores

Pseudo-manners and professional coat checks

It's so easy to pretend

Faking class and faking morals

No one thinks about the side effects

So, have proper etiquette for all of their sake

I'm glad that it's such an easy fake

---

At least it's raining

This place is a mess, and I'll bet you can guess

What kind of hell we're living in

But it's not this place; it's simply my face

# COFFEE SHOP

And the anxiety built within

I'm walking alone, and I'm soaked to the bone

But I'm better off this way

I feel like a mess, and I have to confess

I should have stayed in bed today

But at least it's raining

And at least my world is coming down

And at least you'll smile

When I finally hit the ground

All the leaves are off the trees; it looks so dead out there

Puddles gather on the ground; thick smog fills the air

I feel so alone in this world of shit, but I don't want to talk to you

There's never gonna be an end to this, and I'm lost on what to do

I'm sick of seeing everyone in black and white; I'm sick of all deception in my sight

Everything is melting away from me. I used to know exactly how to be.

This familiar feeling should be over. I find it hard to maintain my composure.

At least I'm lost in this confusion

At least I can't reach a conclusion

At least I don't know what I'm searching for

At least I do not want to live anymore

---

Paranoid

Choose your battle, pick your wars. Close your windows, lock your doors.

Keep eyes behind you, never walk, always run, get a bulletproof vest and a big-ass gun

Close only one eye when you drift off to sleep, buy a safe and a vault to hide the things that you keep

Keep an eye on your neighbor; put a bug on his phone. Never trust your friends but never stay alone.

If you don't understand it, you'd better be scared. You never know what's out there; always be prepared.

In the world in which we live, there are so many nuts. If you see one of them, spill out his guts.

Any signs of fear must be shown, the only thing to fear is the unknown

It's normal to feel a little tense; you're not the only one with no common sense

They're all out to get you, so be very afraid. They even know the day you get paid.

They want your kids, and they want your wife; they want your credit card; they want your life

They will stop at nothing to obtain what they want. Even after you kill them, your house they will haunt.

Don't ever let your children go out to play, because they'll snatch them up and they'll take them away

Paranoid.

You're fucking paranoid.

Wake up.

---

Tomorrow

Tomorrow holds the future

Tomorrow remembers the past

Tomorrow came today

Today went way too fast

You never really know

What tomorrow brings

Don't know how we'll feel

When we do tomorrow's things

Tomorrow's here already

When it came, I wasn't ready

Go away tomorrow

Go away today

I wish tomorrow had gotten here yesterday

And went away today

I wish yesterday was never

And today was my last

Yesterday's tomorrow

Didn't hold a lot of fun

Now it's yesterday

A new tomorrow has begun

Now today is over

It is in the past

I wish it would have stuck around

These days, they never last

# Part 4

---

I've been doing everything I can to put the pieces together. Transition periods are always confusing, and I'm never completely sure of what I am supposed to learn until I've learned it. I'm starting to think I've figured out your place, and I wouldn't describe it as one of favor.

I've always been the one to chase. Drawn to connection like a cartoon character floating through the air to the scent of a pie in a window. Obsessed with feeling loved. I barely even know you, but I see things in myself that I can't ignore. Weeks of feeling distance and in one day my entire perspective can change.

Why do I feel so angry? You don't even matter; I have someone that I have a real connection with, but I'm trying not to think about that. I'm trying not to think about any of it. I'm trying to exist and move on with a little bit of dignity and some long-overdue independence.

***Maybe I need to go back to the coffee shop. I'll grab my typewriter...***

---

I saw this coming; I knew you would bail

The entire thing was designed to fail

Somehow, I knew that, but still I chased

Past disappointment somehow erased

Maybe you were just supposed to be an option.

Something I was allowed to have

It goes against everything I've always believed in

I want to be faithful to her even though I know she isn't mine

Watching the clock and checking my phone

Trying to feel some contentment alone

Wait for your message or some kind of talk

I always try running before I can walk

It's almost ten, why am I still looking at my phone and thinking about you?

I need to understand how to separate

This has nothing to do with you and everything to do with me

This is the last big thing I need to work on, and I appreciate your interest.

Thank you for assuming I'm lame

It means a lot that you never came

I've known for days that this would be the result

We can't stop fate; this isn't your fault

It's funny how someone so insignificant can play such an important role.

***

### *Getting back into the journals...*

This next one has a backstory that I remember, so I will share it with you. I was with a girl for five years, from age 17 to age 21. I thought we would be together forever, but she got bored. I knew she was seeing someone else, and it was destroying me. When we broke up and everything came to light, I learned a few things.

The guy had been in the military for about 6 months; he was discharged and given six grand for his service. He had his military number tattooed across his entire chest. In his free time, he was in a band that played progressive rock. The album they were working on was a fantasy story, each song a different chapter. I was a music snob back then, maybe still a little now, but more-so in those times. Anyway, I was clearly hurt and probably a little jealous, and this is the song I wrote to make myself feel better.

## *Army Elf...*

You think you're under my skin? You think I care where you've been?

You think I'll fall for your shit? You think she'll really commit?

Your ignorance is hysterical; your jealousy is comparable

To my fits of laughter when I'm alone

The dark elf roams the forest at midnight, his armor rusty and his helmet doesn't fit right

His sword is dull and bent; he's too pathetic to even resent

He trips on his own feet. There's a snap. Our noble half-wit elf has stepped in a bear trap.

She'll come and go just like the changing seasons; she came for six thousand discharged reasons

Cocky little fucker reaping what you sow, a year in the army and you're GI Joe

Fucking stupid kid, I'm not afraid of you, more ego than brains, step up and see what I can do

Now that my feelings are off my chest, all your memories can be put to rest

It's been a pleasure doing business with you. You're second best, but it'll have to do

As a closing statement I would like to say

# COFFEE SHOP

Thanks for all your help, and have a wonderful day

---

Ignorance is bliss

Stale cigarette smoke, wasted youth

Weak-hearted, yellow tooth,

Constantly hibernating in my cage, constantly trying to fight off the rage

Such trivial things can tear things apart

All the suffering turns into art

Have another cigarette; the odor remains, even after I quit; the world plays its games

I wish I could smile

I wish I could go outside

I wish I was ignorant

I wish I could fit in

Ignorance is bliss, ignorance is bliss

I wish I could go outside

Ignorance is bliss

I hate socks; feet can't breathe

Claustrophobic, but I can believe

Counting down from three, live and let be

I want to go back and work on my dam

How could you do this? I don't understand?

What are you people doing here? I don't really understand your fear.

---

Recipe for disaster

Starts off with a smile

Bat of an eyelash

Vaporizes all remorse and denial

One suggestive wink and she's under your arm

Last thing on your mind is that you bought the farm

Nothing is free in this world that we live

She continues to take as you continue to give

Something old, something new, something borrowed, something blue

As you get old, you need something new; you're on borrowed time and you're feeling blue

Recipe for disaster

A whisper and a kiss, all the good things that you miss

A smug grin upon her lips, her hands gripping your hips

Such a pretty face, such a warm embrace

She's a special case, so you let her into your space

As the time begins to soar, find yourself sleeping on the floor

You're forbidden to get high; every word from her is a lie

You've done it all again; you put the paper to the pen

Thought she was the best, but she was just like all the rest

---

No Windows

You really had better hope I never see you again

You don't know how bad I itch to get my revenge

In the middle of the street, in the middle of the mall

Break both your arms, give you no mercy at all

Whenever you leave your house, you'd better watch your back

If I see you in public, you are under attack

I don't even think I'll be able to stop

Beating on you 'till I'm pulled off by a cop

I still regret letting you live; there are not many things that I wouldn't give

For five little minutes alone with you, in a room

With no windows

I've been building this anger up for so many years

It's grown so big it's taken over my fears

No one's pissed me off enough to let it out

They've all just helped it grow, gave me more to shout

I thought I was on a plane with a best friend

Someone to be there with me 'till the very end

Nothing can compare to what you do

Now I know my anger's been building up for you

---

Beware of world

What the fuck is going on? Life was once on a very short leash.

What the fuck went wrong?

Did I let it get away? It was here a minute ago.

Sanity ran today

Is it cloudy in here? Reality changed into something new.

## COFFEE SHOP

Is it fright or fear?

Beware of World

Do I need to be high? What's my sobriety point of view?

Talk to me; don't lie

Do I make any sense? Sometimes my words come from my mind.

What's my defense?

Is this for real? Sometimes it seems too easy.

How do I feel?

How should I be? Should I play all their games?

What is wrong with me?

---

Screwing up and missing out, upside down and inside out

Search for me through history, see what I was meant to be

Posture's horrible. I slump and slouch. Try to peel me off the couch.

Sleep's my drug, can't get enough. One more cigarette, one more puff.

Lately I've been feeling like a shell of myself

Misfit toy made by a misfit elf

Day after day, time pushes on. Confused, like a drunk face down on the lawn.

Where's the time gone? What will the time bring?

Now I know I was wrong, but I still like to sing

I crave sleep like a tabby cat; I hit the gas, but the tires are flat

I feel so old; I feel so cold, idled long enough that I'm growing mold

Help me find a little peace of mind, help me out of this bind, if you'd be so kind

The envelope has been pushed so far, in my imagination and after the bar

Sweetie listens while I ache. It's just my head that I cannot take.

Silent screams and apathy, I wish these things would let me be

Like poison coursing through my veins, the numbing happens with the pain

Please help my brain to stimulate; teach me how to self-motivate

I may be awake, but I can't wait to sleep, another promise to myself that I just couldn't keep

As I close my eyes and I drift away, the dreams in my head are an escape from the day

This chapter should be over as I put it to rest, one addiction for another. I should have guessed.

---

Forever

What if when I sleep tonight, my dreams slip out the door?

If I let them get away from me while I'm passed out on the floor

I would probably wake early from the pain of empty space

The chills throughout my body and the stale tears on my face

My mind would do that thing it does, talk to me out loud

You best go track those dreams down, boy, or you'll never make them proud

I'll forever chase my dreams until the end of me

Far and wide I'll follow them until they are reality

Through the snow, through the rain, through the good, through the bad

One day when they come to life, I hold them up to show my deadbeat dad

Perhaps my drive for expression will be my unicorn

Or maybe on the day I die, a faded star is born

If this road takes me nowhere, at least I'll know I tried

Don't stress about the end result, just enjoy the ride

Pay attention to the pieces as they fall slowly into place

Maybe dreams will be a bit easier to chase

The road less traveled may be so for a reason

But I'll blaze my own way, through every month and every season

Never gonna give up, never gonna quit

All I care about now is trying to enjoy it.

---

Sedated

I want to bathe this house in gasoline, lay on the floor and light up a smoke

I'm not afraid to die, because fear is a joke

You should probably know that you can never be the best

This life is nothing more than a personality test

It is not a competition, but a cryptic game of the mind

You could never understand it, with all your skills combined

I feel no way superior, no way above

# COFFEE SHOP

I'd like to be alone, or with the select few that I love

You think the key to life is money and friends

I politely disagree; I am not one who pretends

Build yourself an image, make yourself unique

I'll stay in the shadows, I'll be myself and I won't speak

Get yourself a hero who says that they're the best

You sure can drink a lot, but you will die like all the rest

Impress all your friends with your riches and sin

They aren't paying any mind; they are just trying to win

Blinded by sex and competition

It will never end, and no one will listen

Create your own problems because real life is a bore

I want to be sedated; your "real" world is a whore

---

Here and there we ask ourselves a question

Very seldom is there an easy answer

All the times that we ask ourselves this question

Can we ever be sure if we're right?

Here and there, we look at all our values

Now and then we analyze our lives

Sometimes we all gaze into the shadows

Sometimes we all gaze upon our wives

Sometimes we question all of our decisions

Sometimes we know that all of them were right

Here and there we question our morals

Ask ourselves if we can sleep at night

Often times we listen to our instincts

Seldom do they lead us astray?

I silently fear hooded man on horseback

A hidden fear that any day could be the last

We try to live each day to the fullest

We don't want to waste any time

Keep re-living every situation

Can't keep track of where we drew the line

If you died today, would you be content? Are you afraid?

---

There is a peace in death I could not acquire through life

This is my best explanation for the blood and the knife

It probably won't be a shock

If you've been listening as I talk

I know this seems like the coward's way out

There's just too much shit that I can't straighten out

When my child gets older, I'm sure that she'll see

That it's better that I'm gone and she is nothing like me

Look on the bright side; I've set you all free

The world is so much better with the absence of me

If you look into the past, in remembrance of me

Please alter the truth, change reality

Pretend I was special, pretend I was more

Pretend I never said all the things I've said before

Pretend I was attractive, charming and slick

Not greasy and disgusting, and making you sick

Pretend I held a place in life that made things a little better

But since we know that isn't true, be glad I can't be deader

If I could change one thing, I would pick the day that I was born

Erasing my face and the flesh I have worn

A horrible son, a horrible friend

A horrible person, but it's come to an end

I hope you can forgive me for living my life

A horrible husband to a beautiful wife

To sum it all up in a four-minute song

I was a fuckup, but now I am gone

# Part 5

---

***Back at the coffee shop...***

I think I need a refill of my mocha frappe latte thing and maybe a pretentious donut of sorts.

But first, I will share another piece with you. During this current transformation period, I would be lying if I said the thought hadn't crossed my mind to go back and see an old friend.

A friend that I know will drag me down and ultimately kill me. A friend that gives the illusion of respite, and the façade of remedy.


Sometimes I get the urge to see my old friend

Just a short visit, not a means to an end

It's been a couple of years, and you still feel like home

Comfort and warmth make me feel less alone

The ritual of preparation, feeling in my gut

Crush the pill down into powder, time to climb out of this rut

Watching the bubbles that appear on the spoon

Knowing the pain will wash away soon

Dropping the cotton and piercing its soul

Pull up the plunger now we're on a roll

The sting upon entry is really not bad

When directly compared to the feelings I've had

Watching it drain, it hits right away

I know I can't do this again every day

When I get on the cloud, it's a feeling I've missed

I forget all your words, all the lies that you hissed

Nothing really matters; things feel like they're alright

But I still know that the control it gets leaves no end in sight

I should probably forget the idea and the high

I'm sure that I will get through this; probably won't die

Sometimes it's hard to let go of such an influential friend

The kind that would be there for me until literally the end

I know that it will kill me if I let it take the wheel

But that thought doesn't scare me, even has a small appeal.

---

I find that some poems are better with some context. I understand that poetry is subjective, and the reader is encouraged to pull meaning that resonates with them, but when I found this next one, I couldn't even remember who it was about. It has so much anger behind it, and I found it strange that I was drawing a blank. I think it's about more than one person, but the first section had me thinking.

Then it hit me. When I was in college, I got off methadone and relapsed. This guy saw the track marks on my arm and encouraged me to push further. He showed me how to shoot crack, and we were doing it almost every day. Soon enough I got frustrated with myself and decided I needed to quit for good, or I was going to lose everything.

I started going to a friend's house away from the city, where I had no connections. As I was getting clean, this guy broke into my apartment and stole everything. I was angry, but it was also somehow liberating. I was probably close to being a hoarder; things were very important to me. I am also an all-or-nothing kind of person, so with half my stuff gone, I was able to purge more. Regardless, I felt violated and angry, and this is what I wrote.

The guy ended up going on to rob a bunch of convenience stores with a screwdriver and making his way to jail. I got back on track and started my career. I guess the reason I wanted to explain this one is to show that no matter how much someone fucks you over, if you can take a lesson from it and be grateful rather than angry, later in life you may not even remember them. Don't let assholes take up space in your head or hold you back from your goals.

***Let's get back to the journals...***

---

Screwed up so badly you had to leave the city

Calling here and there for admiration and pity

Think you're Eminem, try to call yourself Shady

You had a little girl, and then you named her Hailey

Now she's five years old and doesn't know who you are

You missed her life to be a ghetto superstar

You're so hardcore to sixteen-year-old chicks

But know you're hustling crack on cell block six

I hope you get Ebola and die

You put me in a place I've never been

Seeing things I wish I hadn't seen

Two years of no trust would make anyone snap

The things you've done deserve more than a slap

Stupidity and anger are a dangerous pair

You put me through much more than my share

You're a dirty whore if they just said please

They would all get a free pass to the grilled cheese

It's been a long time since our time.

It's been many years since your crime

Yet somehow you still linger in my mind,

having seen so many people who are your kind

You're significant in your own way.

I thank God we're different every single day.

You're the shit of the world, and I'm glad you're gone.

I'm embarrassed as hell that I was ever your pawn.

---

Tinfoil

Bedtime makes me so awake, no time to rest, I must contemplate

The lack of passion is excusable; the reasons are all re-usable

I try to give so much; I give it all, just help me walk and stand, don't let me fall

The most important thing I need is just a friend to help me make it through to the end

The tinfoil's filled with little black spots, and my vision's pixilated with little dots

Eyes are so heavy, but I cannot sleep, so much to say I can't even speak

I wish I knew; I wish I were asleep; I wish I were stronger; I wish I had more

They're all so happy, so unreal. Be on top, let's make a deal.

Sink my head down into my knees, body is itching like I have fleas

This somehow feels like the right way, so I'll justify whatever I say

Let's do it again now from the top. I've come too far, and it's too late to stop.

I try to refuse; I try to resist, but within a couple of days something conflicts

I keep falling back. Am I a weak man? I try so hard to do whatever I can

If you saw through, I'd never hear the end, jump on me with no chance to defend

You don't have these problems; you never lose

You're a shallow bitch, but hey, you've got some nice shoes.

Change

Can you see me? I'm over by the edge; can you hear me? I'm screaming off the ledge.

I'm a martyr in my own right, but for a god you've never known

I am sane in my own mind, a place of fear is where I've grown

I'm gonna take back what's mine; you won't get the best of me

I'll step back up to the frontline; my war has not defeated me

You make me stronger over time, leave my head and leave me be

Step up, step back, step down, step off. I won't play your games and your kingdoms a bluff

The time has come to make a change

Can you feel me? I'm always around; can you believe me? I am down on the ground.

I'm a veteran in my own right, but of a war you've never known

They have all run away when they've seen what I've shown

Would you touch me? Or do you cringe at the thought?

Do you like me? I'm thinking probably not.

I'm a survivor in my own right, of a world you've never known

They have taken it all, reaping far more than they've sown

---

### *I wrote this at work...*

Third time's the charm, left high and dry, excuse me please I have something in my eye

Only love can sedate the demon. I guess fate wants me red and screamin'

What if I look to find the cure? I'll be without her, I know for sure.

Slashing my libido, I'm going back into cognito

I need some time to rebuild the wall

You never asked for it to fall

Did you even want me to call?

Did I do anything right at all?

Another piece fell from my mind. If you had the choice, would you rewind?

## COFFEE SHOP

Although the time we had was brief, I never should have filled you with my grief

I know it's selfish, but I wish you'd stayed. I know I rushed. I know the mistakes I made.

All in all, in hindsight, I don't blame you.

If I had the choice, I'd leave me too

I wish that I could give back what I stole

I never should have crawled out of my hole

I know that I was wrong, can't make it right

Do your eyes now burn when I'm in your sight?

# Part 6

*Hey, welcome back to the coffee shop.*

I think the barista may have slipped some Irish cream or something into my mocha frappe latte bizarro extreme. I'm feeling a little tipsy. Fuck. Alcohol. Transitions. Women. Let me get my fedora and my typewriter. Let me assume the role of the annoying poser who is so deep that he can never be truly understood. Let me encompass everything that annoys me. Maybe I should strap some explosives to my chest. Two birds, one stone as they say.

The status quo seems to be happiness. Whatever is going on with your life, if you're happy, it's okay. What does that mean? Am I happy? How do I know if I fit into a category I don't understand?

She told me she doesn't think love is real. Maybe she's right. She says infatuation is basically the explanation. If I apply the same logic to happiness, doesn't that really mean that you're just in the honeymoon phase of your next chapter?

To me, happiness is an illusion. To her, it's love. I would like to believe in love, but really, what the fuck do I know?

Happiness is contentment. Stagnation. My biggest fear. Maybe I'm just addicted to wanting to die. Maybe I just don't want to stop moving. If I'm not going forward, I'm stuck. I don't want to be stuck. So why do I want a commitment? If she commits to me, and I feel love, and I feel happy, is that an illusion? Last stop? Rest of my life?

Growth is uncomfortable. I keep seeking comfort, but I'm also seeking growth. Can I have both? What the fuck is wrong with me?

I want to be happy. I think. Doesn't everyone...?

What could I possibly want if not happiness? Happiness means you're okay. Will I ever be okay?

---

Just another night consumed entirely with beer

I'm such a hypocrite, driven mostly by fear

Fear of being nothing, just like everyone I see

Fear of being alright, being nothing more than me

Fuck, I'm drunk. Don't write when you're drunk.

You're going to end up erasing it all and reminding yourself not to write drunk

I'll leave this here until you're sober

Fuck being sober

---

***This next one I wrote about my experience when we as a society were made to believe that the world was probably going to end...***

It was New Year's Eve, 1999. I dropped 9 hits of really good acid, and I stood on the balcony on the 20$^{th}$ floor. I waited for the explosion. When they didn't happen, I saw them in my mind. I wanted them. What a disappointing apocalypse that was.

### *15 Minutes to Midnight...*

I dug myself into a hole so deep I'm in the middle of the devil

I cannot clear my head. I think I'm in a bit of trouble.

The walls are closing in, and so is my memory.

I love getting high, but I can't stand gravity.

Can you figure out what I'm all about?

15 minutes to midnight, one more day has pushed its way by.

You undress me with your eyes, but how can I get off when I'm ready to die?

Feeling separation from my mind,

Playing me like you're leading around the blind.

Jesus Manson, Charles Christ, Adolph Hitler and a sacrifice.

I am overheating. What do you believe?

I am coming down now, so it's time to leave.

Walking proud I never gave myself away.

---

Once upon a time there were two adolescent boys

They were both alone and broken, heads were full of noise

They met on the computer, where they had the strength to talk

As they got acquainted, they both went into shock

They both had a real-life story of being teased and used

Cleansed themselves by sharing about how they'd been abused

They had an understanding; they both finally had a friend

Conjoined by such emotion, best friends until the end

As the boys grew older, one took a passive role

He still looked up to the other as an understanding soul

The other took his woman; he loved to have the lead

So stuck on domination, and where to plant his seed

His friend always forgave him, still stuck in the past,

Focused on the bond they had, and thinking it would last

The one he looked up to took his girl and moved along

The other boy alone again, his new best friend was gone

A couple years had passed; the boy stayed meek and mild

He had himself a new girl, who was pregnant with his child

Every now and then, he still bumped into his friend

It all started up again, kindred spirits 'till the end

The boys would sit and talk, talk 'till it was dark

Then, one day, they grabbed their knives and headed to the park

The boy was so relieved with the friendship back in Zen

Then his friend got bored, and up and left again

Several years had passed; the boys had kept in touch

He came back around and moved in with his crutch.

As time went by, the boy noticed things had stayed the same

He still played with all his women; he still made his life a game

He realized his emotions, his trust, and all his fire

Had been placed into the hands of a player and a liar

He stormed off in a rage; he didn't say goodbye

And if they cross paths again, his old best friend will die

---

Time

Not exactly sure if you are enemy or friend

You're the sole dictator of the beginning and the end

Have so much respect for the extent of your power

Destroy the strongest steel, or just make the milk go sour

You have been there all along; you have never missed a thing

You created that gorgeous diamond for the bride's diamond ring

The ultimate question, is there a heaven, is there a hell?

The answer lies with you, the only one who can tell

Time – a creator

Time – a vigilante

Time – a murderer

Time – is on your side

Time – is working against you

The time has come to take the time to make some time to change

The time has come to find the time to make some time for you

Take a good look around you at the city

When did it become so shitty?

The sands in the hourglass fall so slow

Slowly but surely, we continue to grow

You are of the essence; you are not to be wasted.

You are all around us; you have no smell or taste

You are a machine; you have no remorse or pride

I wish I could use you to my benefit; you know how hard I've tried.

---

People all seem to be afraid of the rain

People have a feeling that I cannot obtain

## COFFEE SHOP

People stare at me as I pass them by

People judge me, but I don't wonder why

People are a virus, spawned and fed

People should have all just stayed in bed

People are a mind game waiting to be played

People are everything I hate to say

People are ignorant; people are mean

People are vain, and people stay clean

People are pretentious, annoying, and bored

People do what they please if it's okay with the Lord

People are selfish, obnoxious and crude

People are pushy, and people are rude

Without people, I am at peace

Without people, I am lonely

Without people, I have no drama

Without people, I have no connection

Fuck.

---

I remember when Jesus kicked me in the knees

I fell to the pavement, bleeding, screaming, "Kill me, please!"

As I looked up, in my vision appeared

A size eight sandal, melted and seared

It broke my nose, I rolled onto my back

It was glaringly obvious I was under attack

Oh, oh, Jesus kicked me

Oh, oh, Jesus hurt me

Fuck you, Jesus, I don't buy what you sell

Fuck you, Jesus, this is not to rebel

I am my own person and I have my own ways

I have my own thoughts, and I live my own days

I remember walking down the street

He kicked me in the face with a baseball cleat

I looked at him, and he spat in my face

Proclaiming that I had been put in my place

I stared hopelessly at his mountain of sin

He said, "Get used to it, kid. You're never gonna win,"

The final conflict, that was that

He started beating me down with a baseball bat

I didn't flinch; I stayed on my feet

# COFFEE SHOP

Adrenaline rush combined with the summer heat

I got rather angry, smashed his skull with a brick

Leave me the fuck alone, you ignorant prick.

---

You must be me to accept this

You must be me to understand this

You must be me

Unexplained

Played for a fool

In my own kingdom

Fuck this

I'm not a pawn, and this isn't chess

Come straight out and say,

That you're a fucking liar

---

Pig

Little pig, big pig, condescending little prick pig

Fat pig, skinny pig, throw you in the brig, pig

People helping people ruin people's lives

They tear your world apart and then they go home to their wives

Their pretty public face is what they want you to see

But when their masks come off, you see how two-faced they can be

There were more than three little pigs, but I guess it's been no fairytale

Lie your way through it, and there is no way that you can fail

The first little piggy starts a war and throws a fit

Every piggy after is completely full of shit

Every little piggy makes you look as bad as they can

Chew you up and spit you out, right into the frying pan.

---

Nightmares

Afraid to speak

Forbidden to peak

The world is a lie

Why bother to try?

Never get to see what you want to see

Never get to be what you want to be

Strong but somehow sour

Abusing all your power

My body falls to pieces

My rhymes don't end in a thesis

My mind is convulsing

Your face is repulsing

This is the way I will end

At least I don't have to pretend

That I am at peace

And the nightmares will cease.

---

Uninspired by the thoughts of remorse, undesired by the public majority

Feeling alright when the feelings are gone, feeling outranked by my means of seniority

Petite-mal epileptic imagination, sitting tight, wanting not to wait

Can't help but feel centuries old, can't control my belief in fate

Smoke a pack a day, shower twice a week

Sitting too close to the TV

Hairy feet, nails far too long, apathy has got the better of me

I need to brush my teeth; I need to get out of this headspace

I'm standing knee-deep in my organized mess

My most valuable things are smashed on the floor. I'd tell you how I feel, but I don't care to.

I need a nice vacation from this; I need to find myself a new drug

There is a reason and a half that I can't tell the end, but it may involve a .38 slug

Not a lot of people are overly different, knowing that I've been brought up on lies

Even the ones who share my inner passion, I'll be the one deciding who lives and who dies

Searching so hard for my center of gravity

Head spinning so fast that I may pass out

I lie here alone with my head in my knees

While you sit back from afar, admiring my apathy

Who can I trust? Can I trust? I know they are lies, but can I accept that?

I don't know anything anymore

Or do I?

# Part 7

---

***Welcome back to the coffee shop.***

I hope you have enjoyed my early writings. It is just about time for me to pack up my typewriter and finish my latte mocha foamy garbage. I appreciate you taking the time to read this. I was hoping that by the time I finished writing this book that I would be able to tell you that my transition period had come to an end and that the next chapter of my life has begun with clarity.

But... Nope.

***So, one day at a time. I'll leave you with this:***

Looking back at some of my old thoughts

Not a lot has really changed that much

The feelings that came up while sifting through my childhood

Caused me to feel a bit more assured, less lost, but at the same time more lost

I feel like I have no control over my life, but that I am in the driver's seat

It is now November. Dark, overcast, depressing, but hopeful.

I can't tell you what I believe because I can't label it

But I believe it with everything I have left

Things will make sense

Hindsight is always 20/20, and I'm trying to let go

Surrender

I'm getting there, and I knew that this was going to be the most challenging chapter yet

That's why I saved it for last

I am coming into myself; it is uncomfortable; I knew it would be

All I can do is pay close attention

Learn and grow

From the inside

Fin.

*Aaron Lebold - author*

## Also by Aaron Lebold

---

BORN SICK

POPULAR

RORSCHACH

BLACK HOUSE

BALM OF GILEAD

QUARANTINE

GENOCIDE

BASKET WEAVERS

THE SHERIFF OF SALEM

PENNYROYAL TEA

BLASPHEMY

# About the Author

Aaron Lebold is an author of psychological horror who sometimes dabbles in extreme elements. His love of the genre began at an early age with all the best slasher films. Writing has always been something of an interest, but he didn't make any serious attempts at it until 2017.

Since then, he has completed several novels and novellas. His short stories can be found in anthologies by various publishers. Some of his short stories have been narrated for the Cryo-Pod Podcast. His novel *Born Sick* took second place at the Godless 666 Awards for Best Novel of 2022.

Made in the USA
Middletown, DE
28 September 2025